SHARKS: HUNTERS of the DEEP™

THE HAMMERHEAD SHARK
COASTAL KILLER

JOANNE RANDOLPH

PowerKiDS press.
New York

Published in 2007 by The Rosen Publishing Group, Inc.
29 East 21st Street, New York, NY 10010

First Edition

Book Design: Dean Galiano and Greg Tucker
Photo Researcher: Sam Cha

Photo Credits: Cover, p. 1 © Peter Kragh/SeaPics.com; pp. 4, 6, 12, 14, 20 © Digital Stock; pp. 8, 16 © Doug Perrine/SeaPics.com; p. 10 © GeoAtlas; p. 18 © Masa Ushioda/SeaPics.com.

Library of Congress Cataloging-in-Publication Data

Randolph, Joanne.
    The hammerhead shark : coastal killer / Joanne Randolph. — 1st ed.
        p. cm. — (Sharks–hunters of the deep)
    Includes index.
    ISBN-13: 978-1-4042-3625-7 (lib. bdg.)
    ISBN-10: 1-4042-3625-2 (lib. bdg.)
    1. Hammerhead sharks—Juvenile literature. I. Title.
    QL638.95.S7R36 2007
    597.3'4—dc22
                                2006019524

Manufactured in the United States of America

CONTENTS

MEET THE HAMMERHEAD SHARK

Which shark shares its name with a tool used to pound nails into wood? If you guessed the hammerhead shark, you are right. The hammerhead is one of the strangest-looking sharks in the ocean. From above, this shark's head looks like the end of a hammer.

Like most sharks the hammerhead is an excellent hunter. This is great news for the shark but not such good news for its **prey**. Let's find out more about the hammerhead shark.

THE HAMMERHEAD MAY LOOK DIFFERENT FROM OTHER SHARKS, BUT IT IS JUST AS DEADLY. THE HAMMERHEAD HAS LOTS OF SHARP TEETH, WHICH IT USES TO KILL ITS PREY.

MORE ABOUT THE HAMMERHEAD

There are nine different kinds of hammerhead sharks. All of them have the wide head that gives them their name. The great hammerhead shark is the largest hammerhead. It can grow to be 20 feet (6 m) long. Other hammerhead sharks are generally smaller. The smallest hammerhead grows to be only 3 feet (1 m) long.

Most hammerheads are brown on top with white undersides. Their skin is covered with what look like little teeth.

THE HAMMERHEAD'S EYES SIT ON EITHER SIDE OF THE PART OF THE HEAD THAT IS SHAPED LIKE A HAMMER.

WHAT'S IN A HEAD?

No one is sure why the hammerhead's head is shaped the way it is. It might help the shark swim or float more easily. It might also help it hunt. All sharks have special **tubes** in their noses. These tubes help the shark feel the **electricity** given off by their prey. Because the hammerhead's head is so wide, these tubes are spread out. This may help the hammerhead find prey hidden under the sand on the ocean floor.

THIS SCALLOPED HAMMERHEAD HAS A DENT IN THE CENTER OF ITS HEAD. SOME HAMMERHEADS HAVE SMOOTH HEADS, AND SOME HAVE HEADS THAT ARE SHAPED MORE LIKE A SHOVEL!

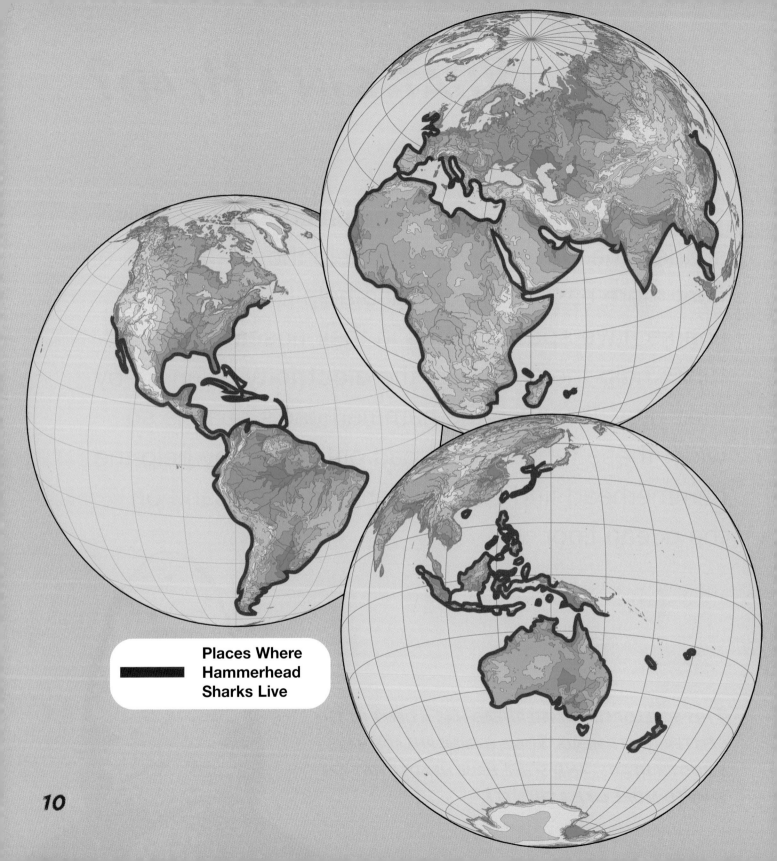

Places Where Hammerhead Sharks Live

Hammerhead Homes

Just as people do, most hammerheads like to swim in warm waters along the shore. Hammerheads can be found near the shores of every **continent**. When the water gets warmer in the summer, these sharks will head north to cooler waters. They return south in the winter.

Many hammerheads like to swim in **shallow** water, or water that is not too deep. They spend most of their time swimming and hunting close to the coast.

THESE SHARKS LIKE WARM WATER BEST, BUT THEY CAN BE FOUND IN MANY PLACES AROUND THE WORLD. HAWAII AND AUSTRALIA ARE JUST TWO PLACES WHERE THESE FISH LIKE TO LIVE AND HUNT.

NOT AFRAID OF A LITTLE STING

Like most sharks, hammerheads hunt at night. They eat many kinds of fish, crabs, octopuses, and even other sharks. One of their favorite foods is the **stingray**. The wide, flat stingray has a long tail with **spines** on it. This tail can hurt or even kill other animals. These spines do not bother the hammerhead, though. Hammerheads have been found with more than 50 stingray spines in their mouths and stomachs!

STINGRAYS AND OTHER RAYS ARE KIN TO SHARKS. IN FACT, THEY ARE SOMETIMES CALLED PANCAKE SHARKS.

13

DANGER!

There have been 21 **attacks** by hammerheads on people. Two of them ended in deaths. Hammerheads do not seek out people as food, though. They swim in the same waters as people do. This can sometimes lead to problems. The hammerhead eats many different kinds of food. They may just think a person is another kind of tasty fish. This seems like a pretty scary mistake. The shark is just trying to stay alive, though.

THE OCEAN IS MANY ANIMALS' HOME, BUT PEOPLE ARE JUST VISITING. SWIMMERS SHOULD NOT SWIM OUT TOO FAR FROM THE SHORE OR TOO FAR AWAY FROM OTHER PEOPLE.

Hammerhead Enemies

The hammerhead shark does not have many enemies. Larger sharks might try to make them into a snack. Other than that, people are the main hunters of the hammerhead. The hammerhead is valued for its skin, **liver**, and fins. Some people also hunt this shark for sport.

Hammerheads are at the top of the ocean food chain. This means that they eat lots of animals, but not many animals eat them.

HAMMERHEADS EAT MANY OF THE SAME KINDS OF FISH THAT PEOPLE DO. THIS MEANS THAT THEY SOMETIMES GET CAUGHT BY MISTAKE IN THE NETS OR ON THE LINES OF PEOPLE FISHING.

BIRTH OF A HAMMERHEAD

Hammerhead sharks have been known to live for over 30 years. Of course, every adult hammerhead starts its life as a baby. The mother shark carries her babies inside her body for up to 11 months. A hammerhead can give birth to up to 40 live pups.

Hammerhead mothers swim to special places to have their young. The hammerhead pups often spend a few years in the waters where they were born. Then they move away.

FROM THE DAY THEY ARE BORN, HAMMERHEAD PUPS MUST FIND THEIR OWN FOOD AND KEEP THEMSELVES SAFE. THEIR MOTHER'S JOB IS DONE ONCE SHE GIVES BIRTH.

TIME FOR SCHOOL

You go to school each day. Did you know that hammerhead sharks also spend time in schools? Hammerheads are one of the few sharks that swim in groups. These groups are called schools. Young hammerheads often swim together in large schools. Adults generally form smaller groups. Adults also swim in schools when they **migrate**, or travel, to cooler waters in the summer or to have their pups. Once night falls the sharks break up and go hunting alone.

A HAMMERHEAD SCHOOL SWIMS TO A NEW PLACE.

21

HELPING THE HAMMERHEAD

Hammerheads need our help. Their numbers are low because of fishing. We do not want these sharks to die out. They have an important part to play in the ocean's **ecosystem**.

These sharks are highly valued for their fins. The United States has banned catching sharks for their fins in U.S. waters. This is just one step toward helping hammerheads continue to live as some of the ocean's top hunters.

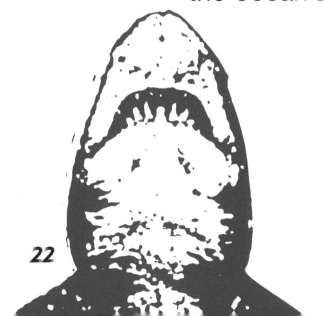

GLOSSARY

attacks (uh-TAKS) Acts of trying to hurt someone or something.

continent (KON-teh-nent) One of Earth's seven large landmasses. They are Africa, Antarctica, Asia, Australia, Europe, North America, and South America.

ecosystem (EE-koh-sis-tem) A community of living things and the place in which they live.

electricity (ih-lek-TRIH-suh-tee) Power that produces light, heat, or movement.

liver (LIH-ver) The part of the body that makes and stores sugar. People use the oil in fish livers.

migrate (MY-grayt) To move from one place to another.

prey (PRAY) An animal that is hunted by another animal for food.

shallow (SHA-loh) Not deep.

spines (SPYNZ) Sharp, pointy things.

stingray (STING-ray) Any ray that has large spines on its long tail that can hurt someone or something.

tubes (TOOBZ) Small openings in an animal's body that are shaped like pipes.

INDEX

A

attacks, 15

E

ecosystem, 22

electricity, 9

F

fins, 17, 22

food chain, 17

H

head, 5, 7, 9

L

liver, 17

P

people, 11, 15, 17

prey, 5, 9

pups, 19, 21

S

schools, 21

shore(s), 11

skin, 7, 17

spines, 13

stingray, 13

T

tubes, 9

WEB SITES

Due to the changing nature of Internet links, PowerKids Press has developed an online list of Web sites related to the subject of this book. This site is updated regularly. Please use this link to access the list: www.powerkidslinks.com/sharks/hhead/